Going Broke: Learning from Financial Mistakes

Book 1 of Money: Learning the Basics

Joseph Evaldi

The Books from the Series
Money: Learning the Basics

Going Broke: Learning from Financial Mistakes (Money: Learning the Basics Book 1)

Saving: How to Save Your Money (Money: Learning the Basics Book 2)

Budgeting: How to Budget Your Money (Money: Learning the Basics Book 3)

Retirement: Start Thinking About Your Retirement (Money: Learning the Basics Book 4)

Disclaimer

Otherwise, have fun reading this book. I hope it gives you some ideas that you can use.

Table of Contents

Acknowledgements

Introduction

What I Hope to Teach You in this Book?

The Credit Card Trap

Addictions

Going Broke with the Joneses

Everyone wants their Cut

Conclusion

Preview

Books Written By Joseph Evaldi

Websites for Joseph Evaldi

About Me

Acknowledgements

I want to thank the workers of America who try to make a living even though it hasn't been easy. This is to those that cling on to a dream that doesn't exist anymore and are trying to re-establish it in some way.

I also want to thank the Late American Dream Dusty Rhodes. Even though this is a financial book and not wrestling related. He embodied when he lived what the dream was. He didn't care what hell he went though with Ric Flair, he was going to be heavyweight champion again.

Dusty lived that dream as everyone would have wanted and he strived for it. We all need this attitude if we are to do something in life and make our dreams worthwhile. It is said that for many of us, this dream is hard to come by anymore. We fall. That is why I thank the backbone of our country.

They keep it going even if our country has a sense of lost identity or wherever you might read this.

Introduction

You are probably wondering why I am naming the title of this book Going Broke. Well, this book is about going broke and I will show you techniques of how to go broke. You may ask, why do I want to know how to go broke, I already am broke, I want to learn how to make money.

The truth is we all want to know how to make money, but most of us in America are plagued with being broke. We have jobs that pay us too little, or we have jobs that pay us too much and we are drowning in debt. We have not learned what to do with money. And we struggle. Only the wealthiest in the world have figured out what to do with money.

I first want to discuss what this book is not. It won't give you statistics and data of how much people are poor and are in debt. But it will discuss why people are in debt and why I'm in debt.

The fact is as soon as you are 18 years old and you work they swarm you with credit cards. They know you don't know what you are doing financially and they know you will act on impulse. This is some of what this book will discuss about.

The other part will discuss about some other financial mistakes we make. This book will be the first of five books in the series. Other books will be about saving, budgeting, investing & retirement, and residual income.

Why are these books important and what gives me the authority to write about these books. First I want to repeat that I am not an expert and I have failed with money. However, there have been others who have been in worse shape than me. The reason why I am writing these books is to implant these ideas in my head and my hope that I will escape my situation and live a better life than I am right now and have my money work for me. I guess this is all of our goals and why America is still holding onto a dream that doesn't exist at the moment.

Everyone in this country got greedy. I am included. In this first book it will be about our mistakes and going broke. First part of the book will be about credit card debt. Second part of the book will be about addictions, such as coffee, caffeine, sex, alcohol, drugs, and gambling and even fast food. All money traps are created through these addictions. The third part of this book will be about the mistakes of Keeping up with the Jones's and why we are in this financial mess. Fourth, I will discuss about poor investments. Finally, I will summarize these topics and discuss about living on impulse and what damage it does.

These topics in this chapter alone could cause someone to go broke. And before we learn how to get out of our situation, we need to be taught about the troubles we all face.

What I Hope to Teach you In this Book?

What I hope to teach you is how we go broke to learn from our mistakes. I believe in karma and a financial system is a form of karma. Whatever we do comes back to us. If we credit that purchase, then we have to pay it back. It is the same thing with a good deed. Sometimes we get swindled. We feel we are helping, but we actually hurt in the end. These are just lessons we have to learn just as I have to learn.

This is why the other person is living such a good life now and you are poor. And other means of impulse as well. You need to not fall for the trap in money and learn to say NO to someone, to that purchase, to that addiction. If you can do that then you are doing for yourself. I learned some of this at 35 years old and still I feel like I am starting over again.

Bottom line, I want to ask the question is that price worth it. Do you want to pay so much and be in debt or do you want to pay the price and owe your lives to a dream that isn't your own. This is something I want you to think about.

If you are in debt, you can reinforce yourself of these mistakes and try to start making plans about how to get out of your situation. This book in the series will start you on that path. So good luck on your journey and learn about our story the American story of Going Broke.

1

The Credit Card Trap

In the so called American Dream we go to College and the credit card representatives persuade young 18 year old people to open up a credit card. Also, they tell you how it is good to have for that purchase you want right away. You don't think anything about it because you get a $1,000 credit limit and you want that Apple Computer that you just can't save for with all the expenses. And also, you are new to your job.

Little do they tell you that there will be more interest as the years add on and you will eventually learn that you start living a life in debt? Next, you need another credit card, that marriage is coming up. Then, you need another card, there are kids coming, before you know it, you are $20,000 in debt maybe more. I'm not even including student loans which are a trap in itself.

Now you have to pay it all off. What happens if you get laid off from your job, then all because of this debt you are on a verge of collapse?

Credit Card debt happened to me. Unfortunately I didn't spend it on kids or marriage, but I spent it on stupid stuff. Stuff that took me about 10 years to get out of and I am still in debt. But I will get to that in other chapters.

Some American Dream, we wind up slaves to our companies unless we find a better way. Our parents warned us, but we didn't listen, we fell into the trap.

Bottom line we react to impulse we are told there is a better way and we do it without looking at the consequences. And with a credit card the damage is done.

I also forgot to say they keep on sending credit card applications in the mail if your credit score is good. This is all before your 19th birthday.

Many of you know this trap and fell for it yourselves. And you know now that you have to pay it off. Now you ask yourself was that Apple Computer worth it when you could have just gotten a Toshiba for $300+.

These are just some decisions to make and all if we can afford it. If we can by all means go for it. If not, then resist that urge or save up for it.

I made that mistake and I feel for the spiritual trap, the addiction trap, and other traps as well. Meanwhile they are making a comfortable living and I am just starting over at 35 years old because of my credit card debt.

I have one and unfortunately I spend on it. I want to turn that around this year. And I am focused on turning my life around in that aspect. It is not too late for me. I want to enjoy my retirement and not die broke. This is what credit cards do for everyone.

2

Addictions

We are an addicted society. Through drugs, gambling, sex, caffeine, fast food, etc. There are addictions for everything. And impulse spending is a way to destroy your financial life. It did for me. I paid with my addiction especially gambling. Because I was empty on the inside and I thought it would fulfill me, but I wound up broke. It is the same thing with my other addiction which I am embarrassed to say.

This is not a lecture of why not to have your addiction, but you may feel hopeless and that is not a road to take. Bottom line, impulse spending is why many are broke. Especially with that phone now, purchases are easy and now temptations are everywhere.

I don't want to be biblical, but Jesus would have gone had a hard time for 40 days in this time period where everything comes about easy, but difficult to live.

Impulse spending is high. It is now easy to gamble online in New Jersey. Do you think they know what they are doing? Impulse spending is the collapse of America.

We all demand a good way of life, but many of us can't afford it. We can't even afford our own homes anymore.

Some is lost with the art of money that they knew

before. People were once wealthy and it is easier to achieve now than before, but it is difficult with the impulses we have.

I'm not going to discuss much about the addiction, but I will discuss about impulses. The internet has made it easier for people to spend. Just with a click of the link and a type in of your information you could have that product. Even with Amazon where I am writing this book for a click of the link and the book is downloaded.

I'm not down playing this system, but it is a good system. However, people have no control over their purchases anymore. And it is easier to spend.

You might think those $2.99 purchases don't mean anything, but they add up especially fast food. It you spend on fast food everyday that is $35 to $42 a week. Think what you could do with that money.

I'm not even going to discuss coffee, because I am a coffee drinker and I am going to cut out some coffee drinking myself.

You don't need that big drink, you could make small drinks last.

We are a nation in the USA that lives large and we need to learn to cut back. We shouldn't cave into our indulgences and if we do, we should plan for it. I am learning this hard lesson myself. It's a way to change my financial situation as it should be a way to change yours.

We lose so much money on impulse spending. We are spoiled and we do not learn the basic fundamentals of money. It's why Mike Tyson is broke right now. I'll bet he wished he saved some money and had it compound.

It's the reason why I am not where I'm at financially now. I can change though and I am starting to think smart. It is going to be a way to change how I do things. And control those impulse spending.

We all try to think fast and are quick to jump at something even if it helps us. This is why books and audio books sell. It is why movies sell to.

Everyone is an addicted and if we don't control our addictions. We will go broke.

3

Going Broke with the Joneses

Everyone heard of the phrase keeping up with the Joneses, well I'm calling this chapter Going Broke with the Joneses because that is what everyone is doing. It's the Apple generation. Most of us have IPads or tablets, laptops and some are an Apple brand, we try to buy the latest stuff which Hulk Hogan would call, "The flavor of the month" as he referred to The Rock in Wrestlemania X8.

However, I am referring to the stuff they cram down our throats. The newest band, the latest thing marketed, and everyone seems to go to Starbucks now a days.

I'm not knocking Starbucks, I seldom go there now. I go to The Coffee House in New Jersey. Many of us never learn finances, me included. We want wealth, yet we pay the price for it in debt.

There is so much stuff marketed that there is so much clutter around and we don't know how to dispose of our technology which can cause a hazard.

It's gotten so bad that I am starting to market my writing. Don't get me wrong I enjoy the writing process and I love to share what I've learned, but it seems like it is too much.

Don't get me wrong I enjoy capitalism and the Information Age, but America has come a point in society that many people are broke or in debt because we tried to live up to the American Dream which seems gone now.

This means we have to redefine the American Dream and what it means to us. The fact is we are not the number 1 producing country in the world anymore and it has shifted. Many of us were living high off our dreams or chasing illusionary dreams that we have to pay the karma piper.

We wanted this and we wanted everything and still there are those that make money off of us and we get mad at them. Why?

We are capable of doing anything we want in this society and making the fortune we dream. We just have to be smart and many including me have been stupid.

The truth is the rich want the poor to see how they see, but there are some they don't want their secrets revealed or it will hurt them. And they get upset at the poor because the poor are trying to attack them through legislation. However, the rich don't take it likely and fight back. They use the system in their favor and should you blame them what would you do if you were attacked.

However, the poor on the other hand blame the rich. For all someone has to be blamed for their problems. I remembered when I was a college student I blamed the rich to and I studied Sociology, but the problem is more complicated then socioeconomics.

I didn't mean to go off on a tangent, but everything serves its purpose and we need each other. The rich needs us to work and buy, while the poor needs people to produce stuff. With poor, I mean working and middle class.

However, we have come to a conclusion that we as a society are bombarded with stuff and have other countries manufacture more than we can keep up with and that is why we are Going Broke with the Joneses.

4

<u>Everyone Wants Their Cut</u>

Everyone wants a piece of the pie or should I say your pie. Rather it's needy friends, taxes, or investment agent. They all want your money until you go broke. They are blood suckers who want nothing more to get rich off someone else's money.

Next thing you know you are in debt for the rest of your life and when you ask for help from the same people that you've once helped or to the government who took your money, or the broker who gave you all your fees they will laugh at you. Or the government will help if you only play by their rules. And the blood sucking friends will keep on asking you for money.

Still to this day I don't like giving money because I've had a bad experience with money. And I would love to donate, but it's not easy now a days. It is when people aren't making that much money, it is the time to give. This is the time that people get stingier because money is tight.

People want your money. There are people that want you to succeed so they could steal your money. And again they are the same people that will laugh at you when you are down.

We all want to escape and have a better way of life, but these added expenses can drain your money and leave you with nothing they can even alter your health. Some people in a relationship will screw the other over just so they have all of their wealth and the other has none. I'm in favor of relationships, but no one has trust in the other anymore. That is why most relationships end in a divorce nowadays and some relationships end in bitter fashion leaving one of them in heavy debt and broken, while the other is left with all the money and they are hungry for more which the courts grant them. And the courts don't make it fair for both parties and in some abuse cases.

This is another area people wind up broke, but that is another book in itself. The truth is everyone wants our money until we go broke or pissed off to do something about it. People like Mike Tyson wind up broke because everyone used him. He had crooked people telling him what was best for him and he didn't know how to manage his money. Meanwhile a great fighter in Mike Tyson was left with nothing and everyone had a piece of his pie that they took from him.

Another case of a celebrity going broke or in debt was Hulk Hogan. Hulk Hogan put his body through a beating for 30+ years damaging his leg with the leg drop. He made millions of dollars and was thinking he could retire with his wealth, but the house was going to fall on him as his son got in a car accident which put him in millions in debt and his wife took the rest of his money and left him. Hulk is now starting over with his life.

There have been many other celebrities that have become broke or in debt. And if you take account human history this is the story and when other people lose something so valuable to them and their life crumbles. In some cases, they wind up dead. They have all the wealth and we see it endless times. Others kill them or they do it to themselves. The wealth is too much for some to bear and is it really worth it.

Somehow people get separated from their dreams. What they did, they loved so much, and now it's a house crumbling on itself because they didn't prepare for the fall. They listened to investors who thought they knew what they were doing and they end up broke because they thought they would make them rich they were mislead just like what Bernard Madoff did to many people.

In a world where trust is lacking in this world and people are getting more violent, safety is an issue. How do we know that we are not next of the list rather it is a physical attack, a cyber attack, or a financial attack. All these take into account why we are broke. Since we are trained by fear and we think we are not guaranteed tomorrow, why should we save money?

This is another reason why we are broke. People want money and they want their ideology to win. I don't care if it's rich or poor or whatever religion they might be. History has proven this in times such as the one we are going through now. There is unrest. Meanwhile, someone gets hurt and that is what this book is about. Why we go broke? And there is a bigger lesson to all of this. Are we in control of our money anymore or does everyone have a hand in our pie as this chapter has stated?

<u>Conclusion</u>

With finances, there are many ways to go broke as we all know. The fact is it doesn't have to be the only way we know. Despite the many problems we all face there is a way out. We don't have to be slaves to our situation. There are ways to make money.

If we apply our skills and earn and invest wisely we can escape the rat race trying to make it. And I know there are many who say money is evil and it is no good, but imagine having that money to donate to a good cause. Imagine having enough money for retirement and not having to work well into your 80's.

The way our media portrays the world on us is that we are not guaranteed tomorrow. We are constantly living in fear and we give ourselves pleasure items to help us not think of those problems and the problems we face.

The truth is there are consequences to these actions. Next thing you know your 55 years old and approaching retirement in 10 years and nothing put away, but social security which is not guaranteed. Many people this age end their lives tragically because they didn't plan and if they did, a stock market crash might leave them broke and they have to start again.

This is the reality of the broke. As much as the rich

have problems, they broke have problems to. And the rich can become broke by careless spending.

We live in an age where there is no control over money and there is greed. Everyone needs a cut. People just borrow items and they don't own them. This is why it is important to make the most of life as it is.

We just try to look after own, but as we have seen in news stories our family fights us over on money and people wind up dying. It is very tragic. Rather it's over ideology or money is it actually worth it. Do people need that hate in them and history repeats itself as it is now.

Don't people know there is opportunity to make money? People can use their creative skills and do something positive with this environment. We don't have to beat the system; we just have to create our own system.

Mark Knopfler sings in his song You Can't Beat the House and it's true. Many people try to go against the house all the time and people go broke. The truth is this world is a money making engine and there are people going broke. Rather than fight the system, we can create a system of our own and we can work for a mutual cause.

A prime example of this was George Bailey in It's a Wonderful Life. He worked within the system and did things legally. He was a banker and into real estate. He made life better for everyone and went against Mr. Potter. He wasn't the only game in town and people had a choice. He was fueled in the movie by his anger towards Mr. Potter that he went to do it better. He in essence in the movie created his own system within the system he had his eventual reward and everyone was willing to help him because he had helped them for many years.

This was a great Christmas movie and it also taught us a lesson about giving, investing, life, and succeeding within the system.

We go broke with our impulses and trying live up to someone else's dream. Someone also takes a piece of our pie and we wind up in credit card debt. The deck of the house seems to be stacked against us. This is why we have to study that system and work within it.

We need to better ourselves every day. It might be religiously, spiritually, financially, and also with our relationships. We need to learn how to live again. We can't live losing anymore. Many of us feel we have lost, but there still is hope.

In my next books I will give you ways to make your situation better. These are ways I haven't fully done yet, but I will try to do as all of us will do. I realize this isn't the time to get down on your luck, there is another way and a better way to life.

If you liked this book please comment and tell me what you think. Good, Bad, or Ugly. I want to know what you thought. So maybe I can do it better the next time. I know I am not perfect, but I am trying like everyone else. I know finances are important that is why I am doing a series on finances.

I hope you enjoy a little bit of my book from the series called Money: Learning the Basics.

Preview

Saving: How to Save Your Money (Money: Learning the Basics Book 2)

Introduction

How do you save money? In my first book I taught you why we go broke? If you read my book you understand that there are many ways we can go broke and you will understand that you need to understand about saving money or at least not spending more than you make.

If you're picking up this book because you need more tips on how to reinforce your saving skills, then this is a book for you.

I have to tell you wherever you are at life 18 years old in a few years this is a book for you. Bottom line we all need to know saving tips.

If you're downloading this book you're asking the question, how do I save money? You have how many expenses and you don't know where to start. I have to tell you this is a skill we are all improving on.

I first want to tell you my story and enforce to you why saving is important. I didn't take the advice when I was younger. I read a book that said at least 10% needs to be saved for retirement or to be saved in *The Richest Man of Babylon*. It was the beginning and I didn't head that advice. I saved, but not much. I am now 35 years old and I made a lot of mistakes with money.

I had a mental health problem pop up from time to time in my life. In 2006 and 2007, I battled two addictions. And I had given money freely to friends or a spiritual healer. Bottom line, I made mistakes and went broke. I am starting all over with my money, with only some money put away for my retirement.

However, I am making changes in my life and I am sharing them with you. There are some tips that I have learned from others and by self teaching myself.

It is not an expert in this field and you could choose whatever pointers work for you. This is how this book should be used. Maybe you'll find that one thing that can be used the rest of your life.

The truth is we all need to learn how to save and there are tricks of how to do it. You will learn it here. Enough of the talk about saving, let's get into discussing how to save money.

1

Basics About Saving Money

There is one major rule with saving money and that is you want to spend less than you make and have your money work for you.

Many people feel the 401K or Social Security will be good for them, but that is not enough and as I'm learning more, there is additional fees attached to our savings that we don't know about. This is why the second rule is having your money make more money.

However, before I discuss the retirement which will be in another book. I want to discuss what is saving money.

Saving Money is putting money aside for another day and let it accumulate. It is not spending it until you want something or absolutely need it. This is saving money.

Why is saving money important? If we don't discipline ourselves to save money and then find a way to make us more money, then we will be broke. And even if we will just save, we need to think of the future. With money we can get out of bad situations that happen to us.

What if we lose our job, we have money saved up that will help us afford our rent or other expenses. Without this money we will be screwed. I will discuss the importance of the emergency fund next chapter.

Another tip about money is by cutting out expenses. This is one that may backfire, but if you do this right, then it might not hurt you. This will be discussed in another chapter.

Another chapter will be setting up other funds for your money. For example, you could start a gift fund, a fun fund, or another fund. You can plan for the future.

The future is not planned for and it should. We don't think of what needs to be in place and we don't think of what we will need so we live for today. This is a poor way of thinking. I thought like this and I went in debt. This is why I am adopting better saving habits.

It is only a start of what can be financial freedom and that is something that we all can achieve if we are smart about it.

This is some basics about saving money. In the next chapter I will discuss about the emergency fund and the importance of it and what you should do to achieve it.

Books Written By Joseph Evaldi

Fiction

A Soul Warrior's Journey

The Day at the Bismarck Herald: The Newspaper Reporter

War

Christmas Fiction

Finding Christmas: The Story of Joseph

Non-Fiction

Birth Order: How the Roles of Each Sibling are Placed at Birth?

The World of Groups: Sociology and My Experiences in Senior Seminar

The Amazing Effects of Water

The Enlightened Way: How the Zen Path Can Help Treat Depression?

Applying Your Own Interests to Your Boring Job: Can It Be Done?

Poetry

Apparitions of a Warrior

Websites for Joseph Evaldi

http://www.facebook.com/Josephevaldi

https://www.youtube.com/channel/UCSp2TBz566yOGiQfLf
k0Zog

http://www.twitter.com/passageofjoe

http://www.amazon.com/Joseph-
Evaldi/e/B00ONSPVQI/ref=sr_ntt_srch_lnk_1?qid=14179608
24&sr=8-1

About Me

Joseph Evaldi graduated from Kean University studying Sociology. He ventured in with writing with his book **The Amazing Effects of Water** in 2009.

He then wrote his first novel **A Soul Warrior's Journey** in April 2013. He later finished writing a book of poetry called **Apparitions of a Warrior** in July 2013.

In December 2014, The Amazon Kindle book **Birth Order: How the Roles of Each Sibling are Placed at Birth?** Was the hot new release under Sociology of Marriage & Family for Amazon.

He is currently working on a string of short ebooks which will be released on Amazon Kindle this year.

Evaldi, Joseph

www.ingramcontent.com/pod-product-compliance
Lightning Source LLC
Chambersburg PA
CBHW070749180526
45168CB00004B/1570